It Can't Always Be Night!

Jacquiline Cox

BookLeaf Publishing

Presentation by *BookLeaf Publishing*

Web: www.bookleafpub.com

E-mail: info@bookleafpub.com

ISBN: 9789363316232

First edition 2022

This book is dedicated to my husband and children, my siblings, and anyone who may be going through life right now with a closed mind and broken heart. I hope my testimony can uplift you and inspire you to keep going!

Wonder Woman

Wonder Woman it's okay,
Stare reality directly in the face.
Ponder all the ways to make your life great,
It doesn't matter who can and can not relate.
Your life is yours, and yours alone,
Live for yourself and you'll always have a home.
Wonder Wonder Woman,
No one said it would be a breeze,
Just understand with the wonder comes all the
reasons to succeed;
And the more you wonder, the less you aim to
please anything other than the word "ME",
Unless you have a team then the ME becomes a
WE.
Anything else leaves for the real powers that be;
Thoughts are magical and they possess so much
power,
And to bring them forth we have to remember
the power is ours.
We control our destiny by what we think and
say;
Each new day should be the beginning of a new
play,
Where we are the wonder of the world without
the stress of it on our shoulders
And as we get older we know to lay it at the
altar;

But ain't a thang wrong with Wondering,
Wonder Woman,
But don't lose your soul by trying to gain the
world,
Especially a world that's cold and unwanting of
a Wondering but a Wonderful Woman.

Signs and Wonders

Sounds of thunder and lightning strikes,
Sundays and sunsets,
We live for likes and regret the offsets.
Of days passing that we suffer from defeat,
We kneel for the aggressor and we stomp on the
weak.
Weeks pass into months, like hours on the clock,
And looks fade really fast, not waiting for
anyone.
Hoping for a time machine so we can pause and
just breathe,
Hoping to achieve everything we want to do.
No one could ever tell us honey, that we didn't
and still don't have a clue.
In order to press forward, we have to understand
and feel what stop looks, and feels like;
And in order to appreciate the sunlight, we have
to know what the bottom of the barrel feels like.
So throw us inside the water well,
And watch us climb out stronger;
Push us inside of a cave,
And for sure we will come out wiser.
There is a vessel inside of everyone,
A third eye you can't see,
Only faith like a mustard seed,

A rebirth from the Almighty himself that's
placed upon me.
And my family, that God inside of us has the
keys.
So to the ones who prayed ON us and not FOR
us this is for you....
If we can take all you've thrown and still make it
through,
This can be a testimony that there can be God in
you too;
Then I pray he reveals it,
And turns your heart true.
I hope the Lord has mercy enough to let his light
shine in you too,
Because I know and understand what that
darkness feels like,
So I sympathize with you.

I Woke Up Today

I woke up today,
Feeling like I need to lay down and try again;
Knowing if I do then I just submit and let the
Devil win,
And Lord knows I won't dare allow that to
happen.

I woke up today,
Having feelings that won't go away--
Feeling angry not caring what people might say
And nah I'm laying back down and praying if
God sees fit, I can try again, another day.
Cause what I can't do is keep allowing people to
play,
And tease and emotionally drain
All the strength I've managed to conjure up,
To keep my sanity
And focus on the betterment of myself and my
family.

So nope!
Imma rest today,
And tomorrow,
And bypass any hurt or sorrow;
But trust and believe when my eyes do open
again,

I will be prepared to not only fight the battle within,
But also win....

Healing

Some call it a healing,
Others call it peace;
I call it blessings when you can just leave it all
for God to handle, and release.
The roads I traveled have never been anything
remotely close to ease,
And heartbreak seems like a recurring disease.
I keep getting this feeling that you don't care,
Which would explain why you're never here;
Anytime I call, I'm met with bitterness and your
intentions are never clear.
The year is 2010,
And I will say this--
I'm not the one nor the two and you won't realize
until you see I'm truly done with you;
God has someone especially made for me.

I've asked him to remove you completely from
my life and
I promised him if he did, I would never return.
What you and the rest of the world don't
understand is
When I promise God something, I don't renege;
I take it as a lesson learned.

Money, cars and clothes only impress people
who never had it before;
A Queen needs to be impressed soulfully,
And God is telling me he has the person brewing
specially, for me.

Whoever my life partner is,
He is still cooking,
Good looking,
And a protector,
But he may have to be saved by someone too.

So I need to go through this with you,
In order to be who he needs....
His everything,
And he will be mine too.....
And we will live happily ever after,
Free from drama, stress, a house, two cars, kids
and a dog, and
A bond that could never break and our days will
be full of smiles.

I know this is my prayer and although you all
may laugh thinking it's not possible, and that I'm
asking for too much,
It's because you have yet to endure what I have,
so you'll never know the pain I still struggle
with;
It hurts to the touch.

So until my mystery man comes through,
I'll smile, live, and continue on my journey;
I'm one hundred percent sure God has a
healing....

For My Son

I feel you in every breath I take,
Like an overwhelming joy that I can't shake.
Sometimes I wonder: What could I have done so
great for the Lord to give me such a wonderful
gift to have in my life always?
He replies "Question me not, for it is I that says;
Ask in my name and you shall receive".
So today Jan 20, 2011 I am happy beyond
measure,
God has given me an unmatched treasure.
I promise this and you have my word,
Nothing or no one could ever bring you any
hurt, harm or danger;
The mere thought is absurd.
I'll protect you with every ounce of my being,
It's because of you, my life now has a bigger
meaning.
Jayden Jeremiah your name has a purpose;
Your life is meant to be for the world to not just
witness,
But be blessed with.
You're the blessing and you will have your own
road to travel,
God will unravel things along your path that
only you can see,
 And riddles that only you can solve;

And he will give only you the tools to conquer it all.

Dynamics

Slam it! Damn it! Family Dynamics....
Outrage, enrage, engage, end game;
Seems weird, everyone's ear is pointed in our
direction.
Why so loud, aren't you proud of our pure
connection?
You have to be firm,
You have to be stern,
When will they learn
That your love was never just given,
It has been earned.
You chose me,
I chose you;
We chose us, and we've been through so much.
Our love has been tested,
Our faith has been gaslit,
We keep moving past it, but I could never play
plastic.
Did you catch it?
That means I'm real,
The way I walk,
The way I talk in my Jlo voice....
So either you take it or leave it--
I'm cool either way, it is your choice.

Day 7

Day 7, and I feel like it's been 70 years since
you've been gone;
70 seconds turned into 700 minutes turned into
7000 hours;
I swear it's been too long.
No one can tell me it's not okay to keep grieving
over you;
No matter how much I try to resist,
I can never forget, or even try to stop missing
you.
You were my heart, I didn't expect you to break
so soon,
I find myself talking while staring at the moon,
And inside of it, I see you
As if I'm sitting here talking to you.
They all think I'm crazy,
They say losing you made me lazy.
I can honestly say it did break me,
I never in a million years thought this is where I
would be.
Life without you feels like shame,
I would be lying if I said some days I feel like
I'm to blame for my own pain;
I feel lost,
I feel like everything was done in vain.
How could you leave your baby girl,

Out here in this cruel world;
You told me you knew I was in good hands,
With the Lord by my side that resides inside my
husband and yes that's true,
But my husband can never be my daddy,
He could never be you.
I wouldn't want him to,
And no matter what me and you went through,
I still, and always will love you.
Your presence is missed,
I swear I won't forget,
And I won't let anyone force me to just quit;
Although you weren't perfect,
You were the one God placed me with and I am
forever grateful for it.
The good, the bad and the ugly,
Molded me into who I am today.

Day 7, and I hope and pray you repented so you
could go to Heaven;
Everyone deserves a clear second chance,
And the life you lived, you didn't deserve.
You weren't given a fair chance on Earth,
So I hope you're making the eternal one count;
I hope and pray you've figured it out by now.
Until we meet again,
I will reach out beyond the still wind,
And find you with every stroke of my pen.
And hopefully you will love me in the end,

My friend,
My daddy,
Day 7.. ...
I hope you're in Heaven.

God Said….

God said "Baby, I'm finna sit you by yourself, I don't want you to get distracted; I'm finna remove anything & everybody- friends, family, spouse, associates etc, that's distracting you from reaching your full potential, anything that's blocking you from the blessing I have set aside for you. You may not understand this and it might cause you a lot of hurt and pain, but i need you to trust me, cause what you don't know is that there's something greater on the other side and as long as you're distracted, being used, getting hurt, carrying so much weight on your shoulders etc-- you will never get there or you will lose focus and lose interest in what I have for you. So I gotta come save you from yourself and others, just be patient with me, trust me, and heal, so that after the storm is over, everything will make sense and you will be able to enjoy your blessings in a happy, safe, and healthy mindset. #BeBlessed

Chess Not Checkers

Those who know the game of chess know the role the Queen plays. She silently controls the whole game while uplifting and advising the king. She knows her position and is so secure, she never needs to validate that she is in charge. She allows the king to be great and knows that his physical strength is needed to win but he can't do that if his esteem and mentality is torn down. He must have the confidence that he can only get from her. The Queen speaks life into her king, not just because she loves him, but because in order to strengthen their kingdom, they have to be a team. United we stand divided we fall. I don't need to shout how independent I am, those who know me know I'm a soldier, but god didn't give me some gifts and I can respect that. One piece of the puzzle will never complete any mission; no matter how many hats we wear, we still need something or someone to complete the puzzle of life. Stop speaking life into the words "I don't need a man…..", you may not need the validation of one, or the heartache from one. But do know that those kinds of men are weak, and haven't found their purpose. No you don't need an average man, a weak man, a codependent man! You need a king, you exude

royalty and that should be paired with someone
who knows what you offer, and has the ability to
bring fruition to that!

In the Mind

Poetry in the mind of me,
I see things others dare to see;
My third eye is always open, ain't no other way
to be,
That's what you'll always get when you deal
with a vessel of prophecy.

Poetry in the mind of you,
You come and go, but to your heart you always
remain true.
No matter what, you think everything through,
And you never complicate life;
That's why I love you.
Kingdom and wisdom is poetry in the mind of
you.

Poetry in the mind of them,
They look at us with a face so grim.
We ain't gotta worry about our light,
It'll never go dim.
No matter how much people prey on our
kingdom.

Poetry in the mind of us,
We love each other now,
But it took a lot of trust

And it took a lot of pain
And it took a lot of rain;
Our forefront was never easy,
Too busy trying to be pleasing for everyone else,
instead of who matters most.
We never boast or gloat, because we found out
the hard way what road that leads to;
We can never ever go back,
Just keep pushing through.

God has blessed us in so many ways,
We are in year 7 and we are in love more than
ever;
Infinity is poetry in the mind of us!

Harsh Realities

I don't like when older people think they can tell you how to raise or chastise your kids just because they have older children or raised a lot of kids (maybe even you). This goes for mothers, fathers, aunts, uncles, etc. If the children you raised are toxic, suffer from detachment issues, if you let anyone watch your children just to "get away", neglect, mental, physical or emotional abuse, emotional incest, PTSD, addiction, deadbeats, if they watched you go through DV and you continued to stay, love a man/woman more than you did yourself or your children, etc. You will never and I mean never have any advice for me. Because the first thing y'all yell is how many kids y'all raised, and my first and only question is: "Okay, and where is your success story?".

Blinded by the Noise

Their thoughts are so loud,
Their hearts beating pound after pound;
I can not overcome the sounds
Of thunder and lightning going round after
round.
The lack of character is so profound
Yet they soar and I'm left on the ground trying to
figure out my now.
So by now I'm bowing out;
I have nothing left to lose,
Nothing more to prove,
So tired of being used,
I have given all I can give and still left so
confused.
How dare they try to make me chose,
How dare they try to cut me loose,
I'm the roughest, toughest bitch on the loose,
With everything to gain,
And nothing to lose.
And beggars can't be choosers,
And there ain't never been a begging bone in this
body;
Only a long stroke from Mr Miagi,
With my thighs up screaming
"I'm coming with you Zaddy!"

Now right away he knew I was feeling him and
gladly,
Trying to play hard to get and
I'll admit I fell sporadically;
Yet to the naked eye and the naked thigh I'll be
Right next to him until
I can't breathe naturally.
He is my flame,
The heat in my veins,
That keeps me sane
And drives me insane all at the same time.

Is that a crime,
If he is gone past a certain time?
I can't unwind,
No matter how much wine I drink.
Or I whine,
Or cry or cause commotion,
Cause his presence fills up my inner ocean,
So deep with emotion,
Beyond reproach and I'm left legless and in a
fortress.
So I must rest, but first I have to pass all these
tests
Given to me by myself,
Can I truly handle the cards I have dealt without
wealth?
Speak it into existence and it will come "that's
what she said",

Shout it out while you're still young,
No need to kill, steal or beg,
Or lay in another's bed;
He is mine and I am his, and anyone that goes
against this,
We must condemn.
We don't judge them or anything they do,
But mfs are so quick to want to know and
criticize what we do.
Like who TF died and made you rule?
When did the lord leave heaven to bring the
gavel to you?

Blinded by the noise,
So we hide our wives, hide our husbands, hide
our kids and close our blinds to the bullshit.
And if you ain't the one for drama you'd be on
the same shit.
And that's all the way 100.

PLEASE

Man please! I'm so sick of these bragging ass
niggas,
With their scary ass fingers
On borrowed triggers,
Claiming they are the ones in real danger
Of strangers
Who just try to make it home.
Some with families,
Others live alone like Rolling Stones,
Doesn't mean they don't deserve the God given
chance to grow old;
This world is so cold.
Stone ice if you really wanna know.

Yes! I'm sick of these false ass prophets,
Hypocritical mfs who always got them bug eyes
in somebody else's business.
Everytime mfs come around, we are bombarded
with 100 questions about our personal business.

We don't owe y'all a damn explanation
Of how we chose to live in this world.
Ever sit back and wonder why the conversation
is different when we start one?

Because it doesn't consist of wanting or needing
to know what's happening behind your four
walls!

Practicing witchcraft disguising it as Bible
thumping,
But the true master sees right through the mess;
Temporary tests will make you think you've
been blessed but in reality he is trying to see
who will pass and who will fail to cut that snake
by the head and not the tail.
Some people fail simply because they secretly
love to dwell in the spell of the snake so they
only cut the tail and not the head cause truth be
told,
They'd rather grow old in a mess, than to clean
it up and live happily in riches and gold.

I'll Never Be

I'll never be as nice as you,
As much as I may want to be....
It's just not in me,
I'm made differently.
They say I'm on something called a spectrum,
I think they say I'm somewhat special.
But my mom says I'm a superhero,
And my daddy thinks I'm a genius....
So I can never be as normal as you,
My brain moves a million miles a minute,
I can't slow down because you can't speed up.
And if you think I'm going to pity myself, good
luck.
I'm gonna keep it a buck,
I'm good bro trust;
I'm moving and grooving on a higher level,
So get on back you Devil.
You can't trick me talking about following me
and I will give you the world,
How are you gonna give me what's already
mine?
That's like saying you gonna take all MJ rings
and give 'em back to him,
The ones he won in his prime;
You ain't got a dime that can persuade me to
want to be you anyway.

I'm comfortable with who I am,
I don't want to be just like the rest,
I'm cool as a fan just being the best.

****dedicated to autism****

Exit Young

If I die young set me free with ashes,
 Sprinkle me on a bed of roses and sunflowers,
Anchor me right next to Moses in the Red Sea.
Send me away with the words of a love song;
Uh oh uh oh
Lord, bring me back as a rainbow so I can shine
down on my mother,
She'll know she is safe and, I'm with you when
She stands under my colours;
Oh and life ain't always what you think it's
gonna be,
No it's not even grey, but she buries her baby;
The sharp knife of a short life,
Well, I've had just enough time
So....
If I die young, bury me in satin.
Lay me down on a bed of roses,
Sink me in the river at dawn,
Send me away with the words of a love song.
The sharp knife of a short life,
Well I've had just enough time.
And I'll be wearing white when I enter into your
kingdom,
I'm as green as the ring on my little cold finger.
I've known the lovin' of a man,

But it sure felt nice when he was holding my
hand.
There's my husband who says he'll love me
forever,
Who would have thought forever could be
severed
By the short life of a cute little wife.
Blinded by love but regained my light with my
wonderful children and a love that's all mine;
Well I've had just enough time!
So put on your best boys and Mommy will wear
my pearls,
What I never did is done.
"A penny for my thoughts?",
Oh no, I'll sell them for a dollar,
They're worth so much more after I'm a goner.
And maybe then you'll hear the words I been
singin'
Funny when you're dead how people finally start
listenin'

If I die young,
Bury me in satin,
Lay me down on a bed of roses,
Sink me in the river at sunset,
Send me away with the words of a love song no
one will ever forget;
The music of a dove,
Go with peace and love.

Gather up your tears,
Keep 'em in your pocket,
Save 'em for a time when your really gonna need
'em;
So put on your best boys,
And I'll wear my pearls.

Facebook Post

God brought me a long way, and I realize what's important and what's not. No one can ever make me go back to who I used to be, ever. It's called growth; I'm a good wife, mother, sister and daughter and if I fall short, I am justified in that. Never apologize for your past, look towards the future and enjoy today. #happywifehappylife

Listen Linda!

I want you to put your foot down with your mate (love me the way I need to be loved or I'm out). I want you to set hard boundaries with people and stick to them. I want you to dive head first into your business/goals. I want you to take control of your life instead of letting things happen to yourself. I want you to realize that you're worthy of everything your heart desires. I say all of this because I can relate;
There was a time when I would rather stay in bed because it was easier than dealing with life. There was a time when I was afraid to set boundaries with people.
There was a time when I thought I wasn't worthy...but life is SO much better now that I know my worth and I walk in my greatness. I want the same for you all!
I hope every woman/man somehow gets to see this and knows that I'm rooting for you …...

My Hero

Today was a hard one to get past, it never
changes.
So many have tried, and so many have fallen.
I give thanks to all those who have answered the
call to fight a good fight.
Not knowing what to expect, and still exceeding
the impossible.
There are so many to give gratitude to, but the
names are endless.
Through it all, Failure Was Not An Option.
And the fight still goes on!!
Hard Rock Charlie 2/7 INF.

-Sgt. Marvis Cox

How Long I've Waited

If I never open my eyes again,
I'd be content with where our love ended.
I would be so excited to share with God,
The joy you brought to my heart.
No one could ever love me like you,
You wake up everyday unknowingly proving
How the next day will be better than the last,
And you do it all with a fist full of class.
I've never met a man in all my life
Who shows as much compassion and love for
his wife
And never takes anything for granted;
He never rolls the dice,
He sticks to his word, and never complains.
And for these reasons alone, he will always
remain--
My lover,
My best friend,
The king of our castle..
You let the Lord use you as a vessel to turn my
dreams to reality,
And for that I'm grateful
And loyal and will continue to spoil you......

Always.

Anonymous Poem

I saw a young mother
With eyes full of laughter,
And two little shadows
Came following after.

Wherever she moved,
They were always right there;
Holding onto her skirt,
Hanging onto her chair,.
Before her, behind her--
An adhesive pair.

"Don't you ever get weary
As day after day,
your two little tagalongs
Get in your way?"

She smiled as she shook
Her pretty young head,
And I'll always remember
The words that she said.

"It's good to have shadows
That run when you run,
That laugh when you're happy,
And hum when you hum;

For you only have shadows
When your life's filled with sun."

Anonymous

Ode to Maya

Plastic women wonder where my secret lies;
I'm cute but not built to suit a fashion model's
size.
But when I start to tell them,
They think I'm telling lies;
I say,
"It's in the reach of loyalty of my character,
The span of my mind,
The stride of my step,
The need for my kind.
I'm a woman,
Wonderfully
Wonderful woman;
That's me."

I walk into a room,
Just like a summer's breeze;
And to my man,
The fellows stand or
Fall back with ease.
I say,
"It's the glow in my skin,
And point of my chin,
The logic of my brain,
As I dance through my pain.
I'm a woman,

Wonderfully
Wonderful woman,
That's me."

People themselves have wondered,
What they admire so much about me;
They try so hard,
But they fall quickly apart
Trying to figure out my God-like abilities.
When I try to show them,
They say they still can't see.
I say,
"It's in the power of my tongue,
The passion of my faith,
The loyalty to God,
The ride of his wave.
I'm a woman,
Wonderfully;
Just call me Wonder Woman,
Respectfully.